Not All Princesses Wear Tiaras

Empowering Kids About Gender Roles

Written by: Dr. Carol S. McCleary, Psy.D.

Illustrated by: Naomi Santana

I am a princess who wears helmets

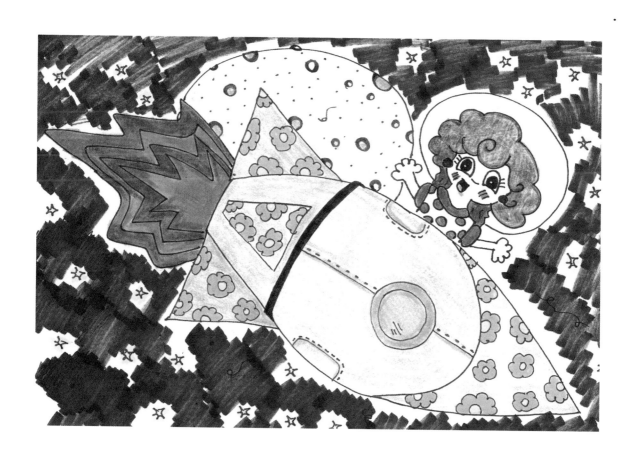

...especially when flying rockets.

I am a princess who plays in the mud

…and leaves her fence newly painted.

I am a princess who wears shorts and sneakers

…to better sneak out on beavers.

I am a princess who visits the moon

…and fights a dragon in the afternoon.

I am a princess who wears a cape and mask

…when fighting crime is the task.

I am a princess who is always questioning

…and spends her evenings composing

I am a princess who wears swimsuits and goggles

…to better bathe my poodle with bubbles.

I am a princess who wears lab coats

…and travels the world on sailboats.

Because the truth be told

a princess who is bold

will be very resolved

to always be involved.

Involved? Involved in what you ask?

Involved in life, that is what.

For a true princess at heart

will not be defined by what is on the outside.

For a true princess at heart knows where the truth lies.

…that to be a princess all you need is to be
kind on the inside.

The Empowering Kids Series is a collection of empathically reflective stories told from the perspective of young children. These books are meant to be used by parents and mental health providers to facilitate the child's verbalization of their feelings and experiences, thereby advancing the healing process and are aimed at validating the readers' experiences and feelings, thereby reducing shame and feelings of isolation.

About The Author

Dr. Carol S. McCleary is a Licensed Clinical Psychologist who provides assessment and treatment of psychological disorders to children, adolescents, and adults. Dr. McCleary has significant experience treating depression, anxiety, behavioral, personality, and thought disorders.

A primary focus in Dr. McCleary's work is the therapeutic relationship. Her goal is to have the individual feel emotionally supported, comforted, and encouraged in order to foster self-growth and change. Dr. McCleary attempts to provide a safe therapeutic environment, which enables the process of self-exploration and subsequent freedom from debilitating negative life patterns.

About The Illustrator

Naomi Santana is a young and talented artist. She is currently completing high school and hopes to one day have a career as a multimedia artist and animator. She enjoys drawing, photography, and painting. Naomi also spends a significant portion of her free time volunteering at several of her local community programs.

Made in the USA
Columbia, SC
06 December 2017